**winner
michigan writers cooperative press
2025 poetry contest**

Prayer's Prairie
Jan Wiezorek

Copyright © 2025 by Jan Wiezorek. All rights reserved.

Michigan Writers Cooperative Press
P. O. Box 2355
Traverse City, Michigan 49685

ISBN-13: 978-1-950744-18-3

Book design by Amy Hansen

Contents

Proclamation: Prairie Fire	1
Compassion	2
Silence Begins	3
Her Two Teen Sons	4
Dreamscape: Ossification	5
New Identities	6
Mercy Me	7
Artwork From a Chief	8
Reconciliation: Artifacts and Repatriation	9
A Simple Place	10
Ground of Our Being	11
Wotai Stone	12
Artifact From Moccasin Bluff	13
Prairie Snow	14
Prairie Need	15
Memory: Prairie Reception	16
Letter From a Prairie	17
Horse, Mat, Spirit	18
Heyday	19
Sludge and Slash	20
With Evidence	21
One Voice	22
Rungs	23
My Father's Cabin	24
Gloss	25
Plow Day	26
Photograph: Destruction of the Prairie	27
The Poem in Me	28
Acknowledgements	29
About the Poetry Judge	30
About the Author	31
About Michigan Writers Cooperative Press	32
Other Titles Available	33

PRAYER'S PRAIRIE

Proclamation: Prairie Fire

You can beat the flames with a gunny sack
or blanket. You can dig a line of dirt
to surround the fire. You can take a train
and flee. And these are your choices: to stand
ground and fight, to dig in deep and deeper,
or to make a run for it. How about you? What
flames flail you? How many times I decided
to move on to another office, college, poem,
friend. When I was at the line of flame, I
remember getting too close and burning
my eyebrows, a singe on my forearm. And I
took to smelling it, the burnt offering, and
burning incense of me, as if there is relief
in smell, victory, prayer, or stink that leads
the way.

Compassion

Hardly twenty, hardly more
than alone, so tired you can't talk
before bed. Digging and planting
all day—corn and apples. Sitting
down for a roaming photographer
with your black bow tie, vest
and coat, buttons. Your wife
in her fitted suit, with a broach
and a cord slung around her neck
and put in a vest pocket. Only
higher, just below the shoulder
where you move forward to hug,
to take her sigh like a face split
in two, with one eye lonely
and hurt, the other, proud, ready,
reaching over these words
of stringy clouds, grasses whipping
your compassion that still salves,
still stings.

Silence Begins

But I feel globular today like topography,
where hills meet a round along
the silence of dry fingertips. Spin one
of your better globes and hear the whirr
of near soundlessness. If only future
could sound so definitive. A collection
of globes—blackwater, as I call them,
begins at fifty dollars, but he won't
sell. *I'll keep it for that,* he says,
looking at his store window like the ten-
dollar bill you were expecting in return,
his fingers holding it tight, not letting go.

The first globe I remember from school
had my town's name on it. Imagine
a globe of the world, with a spot
for a place as small as your town—
we're talking type, font, as well as feel.
I felt it, around it, felt it up and down.
I felt it along the river path, and I felt

the prairie, all its remnants, across
summer vacations, from Michigan
to the plains, sandhills to wetlands.
I felt west to the toehills—as Mother
called them—too small to be foothills,
just the start of a foot, from the toe
and on to the high-boot mountains
on a blackwater globe of relief,
feeling its blessed bulge taking you
places where—praise be—
silence begins.

Her Two Teen Sons

I don't know how time works
to deliver disbelief. I don't
know how night becomes
the horror it is—that they
no longer breathe on this land.
I do know time offered

two teens eternity, having given
them a plot to drink alcohol
and take—no, experiment
with taking—away time with pills
that were not theirs. This plot
is ongoing—experimental
and experiential for many upon
this land.

In time, what I don't know, you do.
Like removing drugs from a cabinet,
or taking a breath to deactivate them
in a pouch. In time, water you add
will make them no longer
what they were.

Time is memory-breath for a mother
who uses a word: *biodegradable*.
She explains with words: *too late,
listen, ask for help*. This mother says
simple things over time, but I don't
remember the images. We both ask
her to take another breath, and one
after that. And many more
for both of us.

Dreamscape: Ossification

You know this by closing and then opening
your eyes: envisioning the pelvis, the ulna,
and many more that gather separately
across a scrim of shelter; all nations of verticals
and horizons move toward you as from a black
sky. And just as instantly, one set of bones
fades, another approaches to harmonize
white on dark, ossified, so you can see sky's
darkness invade—bone to bone, endlessly
moving, art to heart. How often have you tried
to paint them, reflect upon them, sew them,
nail them together in a woodshop? And what
have you captured? Ezekiel speaks Bones,
and a spirit of Godhead moves them
into life. We think skin hugging skin seems
right, but bones come first, before
sinew, and suture, and succor.

New Identities

Maybe it's you I held like a safe flat
prairie, with hope smattered all over
the shag, its grasses protecting us.
Am I speaking of you and me, along
with us and all of us? Souls shine
from clouds and over all pronouns
of us assembled here. Souls, after all,
know us best. Know who is who,
and how to love looking up at clouds
above our new identities. No tent or
yurt, no tepee or igloo, but two sofa
cushions and blankets on carpet, big
enough to dream of self, small
enough to face ceiling clouds over
the light, a full moon, when I rarely
get pronouns right. Metamorphosis
is taking us, transforming us into new
shapes right in the living room, where
living happens: new vigor, new energies,
new spirit.

Mercy Me

Compassion is a sign you hold
all day, with its humble words
from schools, fire trucks, and
flames of sound. Long days
without a sign. Dogs I can't
hear, only gnashing sounds
that frogs make. Or marsh
water spreading into bones.
Aches through blocks, with
Italianate buildings and false
fronts, red eyes, lips naturally
a color. Some turn away, put
up *Closed* signs by parked
cars. My hearing good enough
to feel them locking doors inside
homes, as if I would steal their
megawatts. Turn over compassion
and read what it says—your meek,
shy letters will *mercy me*.

Artwork From a Chief

What is the reality of a living prairie?
Red ground as the field of vision, and it
feels like you are taking chalk to me,
reimagining me, drawing me into being
as the sky I once was. I am embarrassed
to show you my chest of grasses, my
breechcloth blowing, but these elements
spark, as if aligned to stars. We show
ourselves in profile and carry our wounds
in secret, like lips torn from husks and hides.
I cannot believe how red and blue you
have become, taking me into yourself: how
prairie lies ill and waits for nothing but hands
to feed it strength over decades of beatings,
or is it bleating? A sound that animals make
when they sense your hands nearby to hold
them dimensionally. That is why you end
every poem with the word: *fondly*.

Reconciliation: Artifacts and Repatriation

After a massacre, items, bloodstained, are taken, and it does a soul good, as they say, to know they are held—no matter how improperly—in dark boxes to remember proud nations that no longer dance. But souls cry out in open fields like a dark box that cannot hold them. Others write letters and ask that a baby's rattle be returned.

We all know how much we are blessed to be here, in the presence of each other, not with handshakes, but with voices reconciling tonight. Whether the toy rattle be burned, or welcomed, or prayed upon, or healed, or displayed, or carried into our spirits, we know the four winds have chosen to shake it.

A Simple Place

What place names do you remember:
Dowagiac, Oglala, Monadnock, Michigan
City? Place names live, but the real lives
of people who lived here rarely survive
our fragile memories. Are indigenous ones
truly known for who and where they are
along these bluffs and grasses, forests
and waterways? Our borders of definition:
Yankton, Ottumwa, Sisseton?

Oh, Gloria Anzaldúa, please allow spirits
of the borderlands to bleed healing into our
blessings. We move as they do their work
in us. Do you remember: Niagara, Cayuga,
Wahpeton? Explain to me a simple life
in a simple place.

Ground of Our Being

I know you, silence, shunting cries.
I know you, perpetrator, removing choices.
I know you, illness, destroying motions.

You close us from learning, give us nothing.
You trap us with forced happiness.
Unhappy and degraded and depressed
are those on your trail.

Happy are those who walk upon a new one,
where we make our choices. Look for others
along this path.

We will celebrate each other's wonder of what our
bodies can still do. Our cries will be heard.
Lives of poets are here in one body,

holding selves together. We will speak our songs
and sounds and voices, sometimes choosing words.
We still cry and laugh and move and make.

I hear six crows facing south.
I hear trees on Mother Earth.
I hear caws and the healing
of all our family's limbs.

Wotai Stone

First names in a town entrench
their rot in sod. Streets to admire
in a name, names we remember
on a street: cemetery of millers,
land speculators, owners of deeds
and distilleries. It was Father who
made stones first and polished them
in mystery. I am feeling for *Wotai*
—woe-tye—how it touches inside
stony mouth, east of peace, salve
southerly, Father, western-strong,
map-reading powdered purity up
north, cold. But I am still getting
to know you all, being no native
son. Gulls call for me through haze
and circle four steepling directions
on a white marker. I hear sound-
pouring vision, touching porous
luster, asking this town to hit
groundwater. When will stone
drink, telling of all the wrongs
it swallowed for us?

Artifact From Moccasin Bluff

Maybe a bird claw decorated
the rim of this clay pot, giving
us ingenuity—as a bird wing
gives lift to clay, or bird spirit
announces ancestors' brocade
under sun, puzzling sky, running
water from the west into our hands,
as one stream downhill might fill
pottery, where I imagine carrying
it from this hillside, feeling tall,
secreting remnants of Michigan's
notched crock, appliqued, found
only at Moccasin Bluff, an artifact
perhaps a millennium old, lip-lined
by one who pondered a clay pot
and drank in ideas.

Prairie Snow

The antique print—in color—with prairie fire
and train on the tracks. Which vehicle emits
more smoke—the rolling furnace or a coal-
fired engine smoking toward infinity?
Where Father got his first job. He was sixteen,
working one night for the railroad, shoveling
snow to clear tracks. During a break, he stood
near a fire barrel, warming his hands. The men,
old, already there, stood far removed from fire.
Odd, wouldn't they want heat? It warmed Father
so much that, under coat and shirt, he began
to sweat, making night colder, sadder, sick,
and lonely, icy and foolish, with snow down
his neck. His story has no punchline, but his
poem suffers. Endures as spirit does, going
beyond itself in the coming prairie fire,
prairie snow.

Prairie Need

He leans toward me, swaying closer, perhaps
to see abstract expressionism on ceramics.
The vessels mimic rust like hills of prairie
agates, only large as humans. He strokes inky
air and relaxes his fists into two round balls.
Come here often? he asks, like grass snagging
his hair, white and gray as volcanic ash.
I imagine two hands smearing the ground of me
under prairie fire. His thumb touches a well
in my pain, my palm, where he grinds his nail
into me. Moving away, I notice a little wound
that enables me to breathe. *Six times a year
to see the exhibits,* I say, saintly mercy kneeling
over prairie need.

Memory: Prairie Reception

A table slanted on a prairie, grasses exposing
our leanings like a plain of doors and odd pieces,
some tied up, back-to-back on sawhorses for a feast,
no fiddlers, as I imagine them some sixty years
on, when the groundlings of us all run before sitting
and eating gallimaufry-style, with a cornfield,
a two-story chipped white gable house behind, rooms
nearly empty, floorboards thin as a bride's waist, with
nothing extra about—not a nipped kidney or a
nursing home near the state line. Uncle Ronnie
stands in a tux, and cameras click a chorus line of girls—
mothers, sisters, aunts, some arriving in Elaine's
red T-Bird, others taken by a third stroke or a failing
body. Kids remember grasses open as gramercy,
prairie speech, simple talk like fingered photos,
sun hugging shade in shade, and a picture-snapper
saying, *Tighter, please.*

Letter From a Prairie

Imagine three of us bachelors,
sleeping under horse blankets.
Cut sod, slid with mud, packed
tight to cool summer and warm
winter—with two windows
for dreaming. I can't keep
the door shut.

Alive on a prairie bluestem, wild
roses bloom on sod roofs, stomped
on by goats. Lamp is low, but I feel
like moving mountains, Mother.
Soon, we'll have more cows, pigs,
and chickens. Our cold well, as icy
as my knowledge
of marriage.

Send a Zepher if it's for me,
for which I say thanks, without
words to write back. Just look
for my wave in the grasses
of Prayer's Prairie.

Horse, Mat, Spirit

Someone cares for your horse,
the jealous gelding, adolescent,
wanting attention and getting it.
Someone is making a mat out
of plastic bags for your veteran
—homeless, alone—weaving
goodness and a bit of comfort
into lives. Someone has a home,
a studio, where you are invited
to draw or paint as spirit arouses
you—where you are welcome
to let silence do its work. Someone
is slowing down enough to do all
these things—and they are being
done, and we can't explain it—
like a poem that touches corners,
where I kneel to clean out what
was there, filling it with two ears
and two hands—and then using them.

Heyday

All I am falls upon me with nothing but senses.
I hear rusticism of wheels on a road—a peep
not from you or me, but simpleness that I am
after a lifetime attempting to find. And it always
hides from me. The sign says *Abandoned*. How
is it possible that wheels no longer turn here?
Cash was king in a world of action, mishap,
conflict, growth, delivery, routine, camaraderie.
There were other gas stations, but none busier.
A world for saviors, laughter, ribbing, compliments
from just one of the guys. A good way to live
like a hangout for a life that opens and closes—
and opens again.

Sludge and Slash

Looking over a river, you gauge
its flow, moving inches, drinking
down your throat to your chest.
On the dock, someone dropped
a knife, so dark it remains to be
seen, unimaginable as a stray
unleashed. If you look across
from here, water cuts miles
south, then east until it severs
a lake, and another—then,
a waterway, finally breaching
heartbeats, embodying oceans
of our saints—emotions soaked
through. Blue dragonflies patrol
and protect us here above green
sludge—and all that slash.

With Evidence

After weeks with no evidence
of activity, I removed twigs
from the wren house. I cleaned
and rehung it outside the gazebo
near the back porch. It caused
the wrens to sing and, it seems,
to panic. So many sticks to fill
the house again. So many hours
of fidgeting with the small pieces,

to fit them through the hole. I hope
it will be a good home. With so many
dummy houses, wrens filling bird-
houses with twigs so other birds
can't use them until such time as this—

maybe this is the time and place
for birds to live here—so we can
make writing the social act it is
meant to be. You read and listen,
and I sit with you, on a porch—
with evidence.

One Voice

A somehow intact sparrow
on the curb. The distinct
corpus of feathers, claws
like fingernails of a baby,
gray and white grounded,
where emotions arise. No
one asked for a eulogy,
so we'll listen to a hymn
from the choir that's
missing one voice.

Rungs

His face is a long
ladder to the roof
like the face of a
saint climbing a
belfry. His steps
toll against stone,
each one ringing a
ladder of rungs. His
sheeting twice his
size, measuring like
Calvary. But it is
only roofing being
carried, being held,
being swayed under,
being strode with,
while a brook rushes
after last night, and
he still steps. But the
lady next door cannot
walk, as we must
walk for each other
and stoop for another.
His ladder bends all
the way down. No
longer burdened, he
reaches ground safely
like the surprise
of prayer, as he sees
your face: grinning,
caring, blushing.

My Father's Cabin

The cabin of my dreams is a love poem to my
father, who often stood still, with his right leg
far forward, as if stepping on the site, naming
it with a footprint on high ground. Choosing it
to be a vista like Oxbow, its strata in the approach
as horizontal, embedded, how it reaches across
cultures and draws us into its family table, setting
out salt and hard tack. After a cold night, with stars
through the roof, my father rises early, spreads
the kindling, and crackles warmth in us—so that if
we could float love, we would choose to do it here
in North Dakota, with clouds covering our
imperfections, blurring our failures. Color itself
seen through a filter that presses us close to Father
—absent that, a poem provides us love in miniature.
So I cushion this view onto my palm, where dense-
hair bison walk and breathe onto trails as rough
as marbled hair. We all rise in the love of a warm
cabin to hear Father say, *I was born a hundred years
too late.*

Gloss

Water rose up a stream, through wild
onion, clover, stinging nettles, husks
and rasps, entitled to be prairie,

from Great Lakes to Northern Plains,
the land of Prayer's Prairie, covering
body, taller than you, wider.

And so the dental society members
were pleased with the new conference-
room painting, twelve feet across,
eight feet high, the beauty of a painted
iris, winter aconite, crocus. *Just one
more thing,* the executive director added.
Could we have gloss on the work?
Some sheen or shine like sun spread
above switchgrass.

Incomplete, misunderstood, or
imagined, prairie has value,
shining alone like poetry—
every time we visit it.

Plow Day

When tillage begins, other arts follow
is an adage I learned in college. But none
of us has turned any soil on this
Plow Day except what is on the inside,
churning our hearts like old tractors
and one-room schoolhouses decorated
with an obsolete flag. There she is—
forty-two stars spread right across the wall
above a desk, with teacher's handheld
bell, readers and heat stove, seats
and surfaces on a rail, posterboard of *u*
words: *bun, buff, but, cuff, cut, cup*—
piles of cut wood, blacksmith here to buff
his coals, but for a cuff of farmers waiting
for their pancakes and buns, with a cup
of maple syrup that runs up and down
their thoughts, hungry to be worthwhile
in old age like a flag that still means
something—or nothing, young man,
with your long blonde-and-brown hair,
cloudy as spring, moody as wonder, tilling
words you regrettably spoke last night.

Photograph: Destruction of the Prairie

How will a rusted fence of pole and wire enter you, and how do you believe you will feel? If the front loader digs up your single tree, which element will appear larger as an emblem of sanctity? How does the arm of the machine shadow the spirit of your hill of dirt, and why should modernity care? How many ruts converge against your far hills, and which human is looking at the security camera, should there be one? Why are your grasses brown and smoking, except one group appears green under a single tree canopy, being degraded as one body over another? If the machine is dominant, what and who are submissive, and why? If you could employ machinery, what would you use? How will your soul react? Using your hands, how will you resurrect the dead?

The Poem in Me

I heard of disaster. Not as urgent
as unexpected death, but a shot
in your pride like a community
overcome by a fool. Did you hear
the BB gun shoot the neon sculpture
on the pediment? A pink arc glowing
at night, but in daylight, clear as the
drinking life. What remains are
crystalline shards on the marble steps
leading up to the museum's
doors. Media ask me what and why,
how and whether—you know that
sense of losing as you glance toward
the hills, like a sand dune blowout,
where you are fired for saying right
the wrong way—
I'm taking dips and rises now,
moving stone to Stone City,
remembering how it was to live
under broken glass. I see my place
on the slanted sandhills, plants
still growing upright, grasses
rising within, blessed, as you read
the poem in me.

Acknowledgements

I thank the generous editors of the following journals where these poems originally appeared, sometimes in slightly different versions:

The Broadkill Review, "My Father's Cabin"
Feral, "Her Two Teen Sons" (formerly titled "Takeback Time")
Fine Lines, "Proclamation: Prairie Fire," "Artwork From a Chief,"
    "Horse, Mat, Spirit," "Compassion"
Pine Hills Review, "Prairie Need"
Triggerfish Critical Review, "Sludge and Slash"
Tiger Leaping Review, "Reconciliation: Artifacts and Repatriation"
The Marlowe Review, "Wotai Stone"
Peninsula Poets, "Artifact From Moccasin Bluff," "One Voice"
GAS: Poetry, Art, and Music, "With Evidence"
Cerasus Magazine, "Rungs"
The Gilded Weathervane, "Plow Day"

"Letter From a Prairie" is inspired by the letters of Nebraska prairie pioneer Ed Donnell.

Thank you to the top-notch team at Michigan Writers Cooperative Press, especially to Contest Judge Tanya Muzumdar, Managing Editor Bruce L. Makie, and Designer Amy Hansen.

Editor Kathleen Schenck deserves high praise for her insights, suggestions, and clarity. What a pleasure it is to work with you.

Thank you, Paul, for walking with me through life's prairies.

About the Poetry Judge

Tanya Muzumdar is a poet, editor and writing coach. She is the former senior editor of *Dunes Review*, and also worked as a journalist for many years. She was a writer-in-residence at *Kimmel* Harding Nelson Center for the Arts. Tanya was also a college instructor of English composition, creative writing, and poetry at North Central Michigan College in Petoskey.

About the Author

Jan Wiezorek writes from Buchanan, Michigan, where he walks daily among the beech forests and marshlands of McCoy Creek Trail. His chapbook, *Forests of Woundedness*, is forthcoming from Seven Kitchens Press. Wiezorek's poetry has appeared in more than fifty journals, including *The London Magazine*, *The Westchester Review*, *The Broadkill Review*, *LEON Literary Review*, and *BlazeVOX*. He taught writing at St. Augustine College, Chicago, and wrote the teachers' ebook *Awesome Art Projects That Spark Super Writing* (Scholastic, 2011). Wiezorek is an awardee of the Poetry Society of Michigan and a Pushcart Prize nominee. His journalism about unsung heroes has appeared in the *Chicago Tribune*, and he is an arts writer for *PAN-O-PLY Story & Art Michiana*. He received his Master of Arts Degree in English Composition/Writing from Northeastern Illinois University, Chicago. Visit him at janwiezorek.substack.com.

About Michigan Writers Cooperative Press

This book was published in the spring of 2025 in a signed edition of 100 copies.

This chapbook is part of the Cooperative Series of the Michigan Writers Small Press Project, which was launched in 2005 to give members of Michigan Writers, Inc. a new avenue to publication. All of the chapbooks in this series are an author's first book in that genre. The Cooperative Press shoulders the publishing costs for the first edition, and writers share the marketing and promotional responsibilities in return for the prestige of being published by a press that prints only carefully selected manuscripts.

Chapbook length manuscripts of poetry, short stories, and essays are solicited each year from members and adjudicated by a panel of experienced writers and a judge who is a specialist in a particular genre. For more information, please visit www.michwriters.org.

MICHIGAN WRITERS is an open-membership organization dedicated to providing opportunities for networking, professional growth, and publication for writers of all ages and skill levels in the state of Michigan and beyond.

EDITOR: Kathleen Schenck

MANAGING EDITOR: Bruce L. Makie

BOOK DESIGN: Amy Hansen

Other Titles Available
from Michigan Writers Cooperative Press

The Grace of the Eye by Michael Callaghan
Trouble With Faces by Trinna Frever
Box of Echoes by Todd Mercer
Beyond the Reach of Imagination by Duncan Spratt Moran
The Grass Impossibly by Holly Wren Spaulding
The Chocolatier Speaks of his Wife by Catherine Turnbull
Dangerous Exuberance by Leigh Fairey
Point of Sand by Jaimien Delp
Hard Winter, First Thaw by Jenny Robertson
Friday Nights the Whole Town Goes to the Basketball Game
    by Teresa J. Scollon
Seasons for Growing by Sarah Baughman
Forking the Swift by Jennifer Sperry Steinorth
The Rest of Us by John Mauk
Kisses for Laura by Joan Schmeichel
Eat the Apple by Denise Baker
First Risings by Michael Hughes
Fathers and Sons by Bruce L. Makie
Exit Wounds by Jim Crockett
The Solid Living World by Ellen Stone
Bitter Dagaa by Robb Astor
Crime Story by Kris Kuntz
Michaela by Gabriella Burman
Supposing She Dreamed This by Gail Wallace Bozzano
Line and Hook by Kevin Griffin
And Sarah His Wife by Christina Diane Campbell
Proud Flesh by Nancy Parshall
Angel Rides a Bike by Margaret Fedder
Ink by Kathleen Pfeiffer
What Will You Teach Her? by Megan Klco Kellner
Bluetongue and Other Michigan Stories by Ryan Shek
The Mountain Ash by Kathleen Rabbers
This Blue Earth by Sharon Bippus
Upstairs, Listening by Melinda LePere
Twinkies by Kathleen Quigley
The Sound a Car Door Makes by Natalie Tomlin
Brain Aura Blues by Melissa Seitz
Bones and Breath by Ruth Zwald

Michigan WRITERS